Sorry I Stole Your Cat

Thanks for Feeding Her While I'm Away

Marcy Schaaf

This book is dedicated to Lux and Tula, the amazing kids next door.

Thank you for sharing your wonderful cat, Delila, with such open hearts and allowing her love to fill my life. Your kindness and understanding meant the world to both of us. Delila brought joy and comfort to my home when I needed it the most, and I hope she brought just as much happiness to yours.

Life has a funny way of bringing us together in the most unexpected ways, and I'm so grateful that our paths crossed. Lux and Tula, your generosity and love made all the difference, and for that, I am forever thankful.

Your friend and Neighbor,
Marcy Schaaf

Once there was a cat named Delila.

She lived with a family of four.

Mom, Dad, a girl, and a boy.

One day
they got a new puppy.

The puppy ate Delila's food.

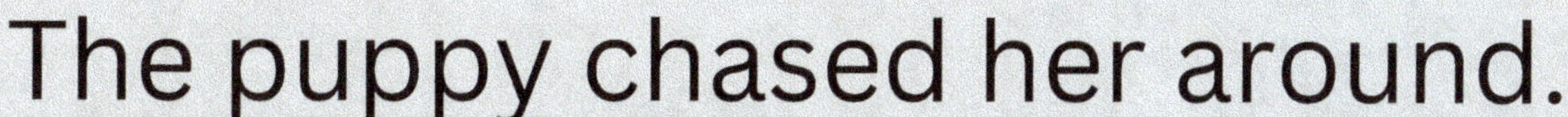

The puppy chased her around.

It even took her spot in bed!

Delila was old and
didn't wanna play with the puppy.

She found a peaceful
home next door.

A lady lived there alone.

The lady planted catnip for Delila.

She gave Delila lots of love.

Delila had a new comfy spot.

In the lady's master bedroom.

One day the lady
went on vacation.
TA
TRAVELER

She asked the kids
next door for help.

"Sorry I stole your cat," she said.

"Thanks for feeding her
while I'm away."

The kids missed Delila.

They were happy to help.

They fed Delila every day.

They played with her, too.

Delila felt loved and happy.

She had the best of both worlds.

A quiet home and playful kids.

When the lady returned,
she thanked them.

Delila purred contentedly.

She was right where
she should be!

Life changes sometimes
and that's okay.

The End.

The actual cat I stole

(and renamed)

The real kids next door

Books By Schaaf

www.BookBySchaaf.com

Find us at: